on Readers

Bats

And Other Animals
With Amazing Ears

by
Susan Labella

Children's Press®
A Division of Scholastic Inc.
New York Toronto London Auckland Sydney
Mexico City New Delhi Hong Kong
Danbury, Connecticut

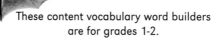

These content vocabulary word builders
are for grades 1-2.

Consultant: Scott Pedersen, Ph.D.
Department of Bio-Microbiology
South Dakota State University
Brookings, South Dakota

Curriculum Specialist: Linda Bullock

Photo Credits:

Photographs © 2005: Corbis Images: 23 top right (Steve Kaufman), 23 top left (David A. Northcott); Dembinsky Photo Assoc.: cover right inset (Mary Clay), 4 top, 17 (Wendy Davis); Minden Pictures/Gerry Ellis: cover left inset, 4 bottom right, 15; National Geographic Image Collection/Beverly Joubert: 23 bottom left; Nature Picture Library Ltd.: cover background (Ingo Arndt), 19 (Tony Heald), 13 (Hans Christoph Kappel), 5 bottom left, 10 (Duncan McEwan), 20 top right, 21 top left, 21 center (Dietmar Nill); NHPA: 7 (A.N.T. Photo Library), 5 bottom right, 5 top left, 16 (Anthony Bannister), 14 (George Bernard), 5 top right, 11, 20 bottom, 21 bottom (Stephen Dalton), back cover, 20 top left (Daniel Heuclin); Peter Arnold Inc./John Cancalosi: 23 bottom right; Photo Researchers, NY: cover center inset (Daryl Balfour), 1, 2, 4 bottom left, 8, 9 (Dr. Merlin Tuttle/BCI); photolibrary.com/Oxford Scientific: 20 center.

Book Design: Simonsays Design!

Library of Congress Cataloging-in-Publication Data

Labella, Susan, 1948-
    Bats and other animals with amazing ears / by Susan Labella.
      p. cm. — (Scholastic news nonfiction readers)
    Includes bibliographical references and index.
    ISBN 0-516-24926-6 (lib. bdg.)
    1. Ear—Juvenile literature. 2. Bats—Juvenile literature. I. Title. II.
      Series.
QL948.L33 2005
573.8'9—dc22
                                                      2005003095

1 2 3 4 5 6 7 8 9 10 R 14 13 12 11 10 09 08 07 06 05

CONTENTS

WORD HUNT

Look for these words as you read. They will be in **bold**.

aardvark
(**ard**-vark)

funnel shape
(**fuhn**-uhl shayp)

katydid
(**kay**-tee-did)

4

ant
(ant)

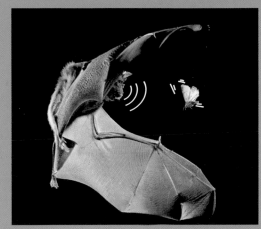

echolocation
(eh-koh-loh-**kay**-shuhn)

moth
(mawth)

termite
(**tur**-mite)

Ears! Ears!

Why are animal ears so amazing?

Ears help animals to hear the sounds around them.

Good hearing can help animals find food.

Ears have other jobs, too. Let's look at some ears and what they can do.

Look at this bat's ears! A bat can use its hearing to help it find food.

This bat can hear very well.

Its ears are **funnel shaped**. They help the bat to collect sounds.

funnel shaped ear

This is a California leaf-nosed bat.

Some bats use **echolocation** to find food.

This bat makes short sounds. The sounds bounce off a **moth**. They come back to the bat's ears.

These sounds tell the bat where the moth is.

moth

Zoom! The bat finds the moth.

Don't worry, sometimes a moth can fool a bat.

It has a special organ that helps it hear bat sounds.

Then the moth can fly away from the bat.

How do **katydids** hear each other? They have ears on their legs!

They use their ears to hear each other's songs.

ear

A katydid rubs its wings together to sing.

Good hearing can help an **aardvark** find food.

Aardvarks can hear **ants** and **termites** moving on the forest floor.

Yum!

ant

termite

This aardvark is looking for food.

Elephants use their ears to do more than hear.

Some elephants live in hot, dry places.

They flap their ears to cool off.

ears

What a way to stay cool!

A BAT USES ITS EARS!

1···
It is nighttime. Soon this bat will leave its roost, or home, to find food.

2···
The bat finds moths to eat. How did it find them in the dark? It used its ears to hear them!

3····
The bat makes sounds that bounce off the moths. The sounds come back to the bat's ears. Will this moth get away?

5

Time for dinner!
The bat catches the
moth. Yum!

4

The bat flies after the
moth. The moth tries
to get away.

YOUR NEW WORDS

aardvark (**ard**-vark) an African mammal with a long sticky tongue

ant (ant) a small insect that lives with lots of other ants in a colony

echolocation (eh-koh-loh-**kay**-shuhn) use of sound to find objects like food

funnel shape (**fuhn**-uhl shayp) a shape that is like a cone

katydid (**kay**-tee-did) a large green insect that is like a grasshopper

moth (mawth) an insect that is like a butterfly

termite (**tur**-mite) an insect that eats wood

THESE ANIMALS HAVE AMAZING EARS, TOO!

fox

gerenuk

hippo

rabbit

INDEX

FIND OUT MORE

Book:

Whose Ears Are These?: A Look at Animal Ears–Short, Flat, and Floppy by Peg Hall, Picture Window Books, 2003

Website:

Big Ears, Small Ears
http://www.greenscreen.org/newsletter/articlesjr/BigEars.html

MEET THE AUTHOR:

Susan Labella is a writer of books, articles, and magazines for kids. She is the author of other books in the Scholastic News Nonfiction Readers series. She lives in Connecticut.